Helen Boyles

Transitions

Indigo Dreams Publishing

First Edition: Transitions
First published in Great Britain in 2017 by:
Indigo Dreams Publishing Ltd
24 Forest Houses
Halwill
Beaworthy
EX21 5UU
www.indigodreams.co.uk

Helen Boyles has asserted her right under the Copyright, Designs and Patents Act 1988 to be identified as the author of this work.
©2017 Helen Boyles

ISBN 978-1-910834-68-8

British Library Cataloguing in Publication Data. A CIP record for this book can be obtained from the British Library.

Designed and typeset in Palatino Linotype by Indigo Dreams. Cover design by Ronnie Goodyer at Indigo Dreams

Printed and bound in Great Britain by 4edge Ltd.

Papers used by Indigo Dreams are recyclable products made from wood grown in sustainable forests following the guidance of the Forest Stewardship Council.

To my 'beloved engineer' husband, Richard, who has listened patiently to many of my poems over the years!

Acknowledgements

For poems published in this collection, thanks to:
Acumen for 'Talisman', and 'Teenage Metamorphosis' in the
Torbay Poetry Competition publication, *Making a Splash;*
The Dawntreader for 'Ted Hughes' Memorial' and 'Nightjars'.

Acknowledgements, also, to the supportive community and
committee of *Moor Poets*, poetry-loving friends and family.

Also by Helen Boyles:

Catching Light

CONTENTS

Movements in nature

Movements in people's lives

Movements in history

Transitions

Movements in nature

Waking
For Kay

Eyes shining, she told how,
one day, far in the Spanish south
she woke before dawn,
watched as the sun
heaved light above land's rim
to slowly claim the sky,
told how, from the world's edge
it seemed, dark shapes emerged
across the fanned space,
gained size and shape and speed
as horses loosened from sun's chariot
to toss and drum the startled plain.
Impetuous, out-chasing day and
streaming its birth fires they
tore from their harnesses,
raced and plunged new colours
in the waiting waters of the lake
where they stood, steam
curling off their flanks,
suddenly still.
It seemed they came from nowhere,
she said: 'I felt like crying,
it was like a dream;
they were wild, quite wild,
that was the special thing.'

Spring

The dancers stir and whisper
in the wings;
their rehearsal dress
hangs loose, a little limp,
but bright.
Then light beckons them
to lift, spread skirts
of rinsed green in the sun's eye
to the applause of birds,
the percussion of the rain,
the soft attention of the bees.

Autumn

Caught on the wing, the still tree
is surprised by flocks of tiny visitors
on autumn flights of busy foraging.
Its height and spread is now
a-twitch and twitter with quick,
dipping silhouettes and tail flick,
peeping and chinking
with their sprinkled bells,
sleeping brown of branches
lit with slips of gold and pink,
candled with their fleeting flame.

Winter

Sleeping pools of waders
stir to rising mist and nudging prow,
ripple a skein of black stars
on the sky's lift, gather
to a wave that curls, sweeps
and turns in the sun's eye,
dissolves to light.

Writing in the dark

Filaments of cyclamen
erupt from swaddled corms,
unravelling, entwine and travel
through the moist dark.
They are discreet, mysterious,
surprising us in autumn
with mottled banners
clustering round tree boles
and in shaded spots,
flirting with light.
Singly and in company,
they prick out shining bracts
in white, cerise.
Ear sharpens to the whispers
of their secret passaging,
their knowledge of the dark,
slow sipping of the nutrients
indrawing as they stretch, swell,
break at last into our sphere of sight.
Mind fingers the braille
of their blind script, tracing
a subtle manuscript of hope.

Cultivating Butterflies

We try to taper fingers to extract the seeds
from drooping heads of vetch,
hold them softly in the basket of our palms
into the quarried space where butterflies are born,
but they are fragile and we need to nurture them
with gifts of seed for infant food.
We extend our finger tips to ring each bed of vetch
with tiny stones, tunnel sight
to peer through a forest of succulents,
tiptoe round so not to crush rare lichen beds
that crisp the limestone floor.

Seasons pass, now we are back again
to watch their metamorphosis in shape and time,
narrow eyes again to spot the larvae
curled round sepals of the finished blooms.
Tucked there are pulses tiny as a seed
we need to quicken to.
They cling there in patience within
and outside time, hang on the season's edge
in meditative secrecy, whisper of wings
in a beating purse that one day
opens to a flicker of the palest blue.
It will happen, but we cannot hurry its maturity;
we must slow to another time,
shrink to a different state,
seed in the thin soil where miracles uncurl.

Acorn Catchers

English oak carved rafters in our homes,
broad-shouldered, bore our jobs and trade and travel,
thrust masts through cloud
to launch flotillas on the island seas,
witnessed the death of generals,
stripped strength for our service,
through seasons hosted festivals
of micro-beasts to burrow in its limbs,
drain sap, thrive in its sanctuary.
Groans of felled or wounded frames
split wooded silences,
sky swam into the opened space.

Shrewd-eyed, sharp-suited, from the wings,
the jay watched:
squirrels watched the jay
saw where acorns plumped
onto the ground beneath the canopy,
seized them for a winter cache.
Unlike squirrel rivals, jay pirates
never nipped the growing point,
but unlike squirrels, short on memory
for hiding spots, their bounty slept
forgotten, overlooked by bird or beast,
yet touched by sun.

Through turning light the acorn swells
to burst its coat and raise its flag
to sun and space. It frills, unfurls
too soon, too quick, too green
for acorn thieves, survives to plant
new footsteps for the striding oak
to fly its banners once again,
reclaim England's landscape,
reclaim history.

The sky has no borders

The sky has no borders
for those with wings,
the birds;
they glide or tumble
in its vastnesses,
flicker
in its envelope of blue.
They read and measure
its expanses
across continents
answering the pull
of earth and tides
with senses we have lost
or never knew.

From high our earth
is small.
Beating tracks
across the wilderness,
sky-travellers see ships
struggle on the waves,
slim-slip past the weight
of aeroplanes,
glimpse the flailing arms
of wind farms
desperate to catch and hold
the movement of the air.

From above they see
our grid of walls,
see their smoking breaches,
hear the muffled hammering
and whine of missiles,
border checkouts bristling:
see and ignore,
move on.

We look up at their shapes
and patterning,
screw our eyes to make them out:
wonder, speculate,
resent.
We try to claim their world
as military air-space, no-fly zones,
aim our guns,
gather force to pick them out
and bring them down.

But still they hold
the kingdom of the sky
to beat their homing course,
follow in each other's slipstream
steadily,
eyes and pulses
trained to other purposes
and distances.

Looking to Iceland

On the northland spaces
of the outer isles we felt
the edge of your cold, the whip
of sails that cut the world's edge.
We were grazed by the wing of flight
to other vastnesses,
drew on the fires that seethed
beneath your bitter crust.
We felt your white clouds
turn in our mind, twist
the iris of the day's blue.
Weapons of change sharpened,
flashed in a new light.
Land of collisions, opposites,
extremes, slow mounting of rock
to new contours, silhouettes;
we struggled with your forces,
learnt from you.
We will tune to the thud of your heart
in our drowned sleep,
dig dark in the kistvaens
of shared memory
to find ourselves again.

Collision

Brave new road
slicing the old green of the hill
bristling with artificial light.
Confident, relaxed, we
seize the space, the speed
of the return night road
till thud and shock of impact,
metal against flesh and bulk
of some late creature
ambling out across a carriageway
that had been grass and safety
not so long ago:
a badger, stained with soil's rust
following ancestral trackways
blindly, stubbornly.

That violent meeting
jolts us to grief, to shame
at the heedless pace
that tears their slow rhythms,
tosses and throws out to the margins
of our rushed lives these creatures
of our shared dark, shared past,
as obstructions, accidental waste,
so much collateral.

Nightjars

Tucked in the twilight corner
of the wood
a swathe of heath
thickens, deepens
to wakening.
Darkness stoops
to lift secrets
from its bristling bed,
unwraps wings,
loosens throats
to a long low unravelling
unspooling stillnesses.
Shapes separate
from bracken brush
and raise slim silhouettes
from legend into vision
in a noiseless dance
across sky's indigo.

We stand spellbound
in the moon's gaze
as muffled wing pulse
beats around
the charmed space
sharing codes of wing clap,
flash and dive,
tranced moths gliding
into hunter's gapes.

We are outside that circle
but can just remember
the way in
across the misting combe
by sunken paths
in some folk narrative.

Eyes widen with the moon's disc...
then we collect ourselves,
rearrange our faces,
remove our hands
from the gate latch,
repack cameras and binoculars,
stumble back
to the waiting car
and homeward tarmac way.

But inside, a different quietness.

Tolstoy's Wolf
Based on an episode in 'War and Peace'

She was old, had been hunted
many times, grown in the cunning
of the chase. She knew
the ways of men, their dark eyes,
had outfaced them in each season's sport.
She cubbed again this spring,
still had milk in her old dugs,
reared five.

The word got out:
the trophy challenge of the year;
forces were combined to bring her down,
the cubs as well. The finest livery
and horsemanship were on display.

She tested, drew them narrow ways
through rough and steep;
they tried to keep her from the wood,
the refuge of the den.
She fought off the dogs,
slipped off again,
outloped their racing elegance
until the hunters closed from both sides,
steeled for the last reckoning.

She held her ground
but she was old, fell
to a struggle and a bloody
nemesis. They wedged a stick
to prise apart her snarling jaws,
bound legs and slung her
on the horse's back,
toasted their success,
carried her in triumph home.

Solar Hunt

(Norwegian myth explained solar eclipse as the sun being hunted and eaten by wolves)

Today, on morning sky,
a shadow pack of wolves
pursued the sun,
with smothered pad and voice
beneath their wild mane,
caught up,
bit into its flank,
munched its pale globe
to a smile of pearl,
scooped its contours
to a curved boat
poised on a clouding sea,
with predatory night jaws
carved light to the shining crescent
of the virgin hunter's bow
taut for combat, proud
and poised to send the darkness
racing back again.

Lilliputians

Clumsy Gulliver, large-footed, curious,
sporting a three-cornered hat
of sky, cravat froth of cloud,
I gaze down at a winged community
of flashy citizens
in furred or glinting armoury
in, out, around
their tiered pagoda towers
of sun and rain-lush greenery.

They are visiting the summer sprawl
of marsh pinks:
woundwort, hemp agrimony,
codlins and cream beside the stream.
In humming concentration
on their foraging, they rummage
through the silken packaging
with footfall light as dew,
with sinuous and whittled instruments
that deftly mine reserves of gold.
Nimble, sharp, they do not notice me,
they care for nothing
but the jewels in the caves
beyond our reach.

Busy mesh of wings and voices
burrs ear's listening shell,
furs the stillness of the afternoon;
wound in a dream of sip and feed
they hang on velvet lips
to draw their sweets
and pack them on neat flanks
to line the beds of housemaids,
waiting girls and queens.
They register me absently,
absorbed, oblivious.

What if they were suddenly
to swivel sights,
and swift and neat in unison
enmesh me in their web of sound,
in murmured conference
decide my fate,
embroider me with stings
and lash me to the ground
with sticky threads
too subtle strong to break.
I can see my human walls
collapsed to siege,
their height and weight
clean-felled to helplessness,
no wings to lift me to escape,
to flee the citizens' united will,
their memories of plunder
and of poisoning,
all seeing eyes and weaponry.

I shall view them
through a safe, protective lens,
through my binoculars,
admire their skill, efficiency,
their self-sufficiency,
take care not to interrupt
their purpose, or impinge
on their periphery,
then, softer than a stamen rustle,
tiptoe off.

Foundry Wood, Leamington Spa

The town was founded on water
bubbling into Spa
then iron
hacked, smelted, moulded
running hot to forge rails
opening new worlds
beyond its elegant perimeters.
Woods rang
with the harsh percussion
of its metal tongues,
hissed with fire and steam,
heaved with muscle clench
and strike.

Then the pace slowed,
pressure eased,
railway speed outstripped
by new technologies.
Hulks of engine carriages
decayed to skeletons,
shed vertebrae that stained
to ochre in the long grass,
railway sleepers
rusting in damp skirts
of ladies' bedstraw
and of clematis.

But it has been refounded
on thin scatterings
of blown chance
from embankment seeds,
driftings of ash
from redundant fires and sidings,
sprung to new communities
of plants, of bees
and human visitors.

In this abandoned triangle
of spent ground
between old railway
and new superstore
butterflies are fashioned
from bent willow whips
and raffia,
hung in the vacant windows
of old railway sheds,
over flocks of viper's bugloss
flicker into colour
and to life.
Now carriages are schoolrooms,
there are tree-stump rings
for story-telling,
sculpted wood eggs nestling
amongst sprouting trees,
lessons to be taught
and learned:
growth
loss
change
refounding
rediscovery.

Full Moon on Christmas Eve 2015

Wild moon riding high
speeds through torn cloud
into a stillness of pooled ink,
carries the glamour
of myth, the grandeur
of cosmic coincidence.
Poised on the edge of storm,
it glides from darker restlessness
to peace, and in its rising
on this Holy night,
sloughs its demon cloak
to shed a kind of grace.

The techno-neons of our motor-whittled way
cannot compete, cannot eclipse
this patient, ancient sign;
we ride home to its steady eye,
borne on its shoulder
and the arc of promised meeting
between night and day
to a final space of moonstruck
hush and dark
and a single blackbird
singing the moon's light.

Movements in people's lives

Teenage Metamorphosis

Now the beasts growl from behind closed doors,
wallow in the fetid warmth of guarded dens,
scowl through cracks, fling out a challenge
if we, the excluded, dare to infringe their privacy.
We cultivate a wariness: the male of the species,
rough-musked, bristles in a spiky pelt,
the female, silky-coated, struts in preened plumes
but with swift flicking tongue and flashing eye:
Private space: Keep out. And that includes Mum!
We try to placate, to reason, then scuttle
to escape a savaging, hover, anxious, in the kitchen
for when the lords emerge to prowl and scavenge
amongst breakfast crumbs.

What dread metamorphosis is this?
Where is that Arcadia of infant innocence?
Winsome cubs at one time, they had gambolled
in the sun, frolicked at our sides, listened, rapt,
to homespun fantasies, rested in the arc
of our protecting arm.

We learn humility, and gratitude, cherish
the gift of rare companionship, learn to smother
pleasure in a show of nonchalance
when they honour us with favour,
slip an arm in ours.
Because of course they will retreat again
to sprawl and glower in their caves,
move to the hunting rhythms
of the chase and kill or conquest
throbbing in stereophonic energy.

We learn our place, manning sentry positions
behind the lines, weathering the turbulence,
waiting in patience for the enemy's retreat,
for the allies to return, relieve our solitude.

Motherhood

Tentative at first
you step out on the causeway
to the island,
pace your domain,
embrace the view,
hail the mainland cheerfully.

You unfold your belongings,
make a home,
plant its boundaries
with colours and with stories,
float the mind's adventure
out on the bright sea
but frame a structure
for security.
You cultivate a new identity,
new purposes,
another usefulness.

It is wanted, needed
only for so long.
Clouds glide across the sun;
in years' unravelling,
you hear the rip tide roar,
winds test the moorings,
windows rattle in their frames
but you manage the transition -
think you do.
Gradually the land mass shifts
beneath your sleep
as settled levels start to lift,
fold, crack apart,
fragment to new shapes
that fresh currents bear away.

It can be difficult to make them out
sometimes,
but they are there
on the horizon's spread
and can ride back
on homing currents
now and then, be
tossed back unexpectedly.
You may feel rinsed
with silence
and with emptiness

But also light.
The planted rows will fade
and shrink back
to their beds,
but you are free,
can try your step again,
throw a bridge out boldly
to the waiting shore.

Talisman

Foxes were your favourite animal:
keen, knowing, bright and restless,
just like you.
You told him how you loved them
and he, because he loved you,
bought you one, wood carved.
He was a gentler kind of animal,
this man of yours,
a friendly dog, hearth-loving,
too comfortable for you perhaps.

You placed the fox
bold on the mantelpiece.
Though trapped in wood,
its wild flame burned with yours
in that domestic space.

There over months, then years
it watched you pass,
and touch, and laugh, and love,
and quarrel, part,
come close again.
Maybe it knew more than you
about yourselves.
With hunter's eyes it bored
the missed steps in your dance,
breaks in the rhythm of your days.

Now interiors are rearranged,
the light falls differently
on objects strange and known
in new relationships.
But pricked in silhouette
on cleared ground
the fox still sits

and guards its flame,
catches energy,
vigilant, still holds its space
and yours.

The Philosopher's Bowl

For my daughter

*Sixteenth-century Japanese philosopher, Rikyu, said of a perfect bowl which
had been shattered and reassembled: 'Now it is magnificent'.*

We try to mould the clay
to fit our mind's shape
of perfection,
knead and roll and round it
to a classic bowl,
smooth the seals and edges
for a flawless skin.
We place it on a surface
polished to reflect its light.
Balanced there, it
pleases with its grace,
draws eyes
but is precarious.

Your eyes had always caught
the bright shards flung by sea
on sand, what they
flashed back of other stories,
other lives.
You had fingered, gathered,
fashioned them as amulets
netted in gold filigree.

When your bowl trembles
and fragments beneath the shocks
and pressures of the passing day,
the stump of feet and lifted voice,
you can collect the scattered parts,
read in them other shapes
to fit together in another whole,
another truth, stroke seams

to find the singing point
at which the bowl's curved space
can answer the vibration
of a different signature.

A Cornet and Accordion
(in memory of my grandfather and great-grandfather)

For years they had coaxed tunes
from wood and string,
tested pauses, measured pace,
felt the rhythms and the resonance
of old themes,
father, son, through time
attending the same score.
They blended chords in private
or in social space,
leisured afternoons
tuned on the public stand
or in the drawing room
with quiet voices over tea
at the Salvation Army hall,
secure in pride of uniform,
watched by texts of service
and of peace.

Another world,
another post,
drivers on the fighting lines
measuring the pauses,
stops and runs,
still with accordion
and cornet tuned
and rubbed, preserved
for different purposes,
another space.
Now the instruments
unfold the contours
of the Marseillaise
to French troops lined up
for the last climb
and descent.

Heads bowed, they wait
for their last call to arms
on concert and accordion,
its theme of freedom
and of brotherhood,
chiming voices, chink of glasses
sunk to the grumble
of the guns,
last notes echoing
and splintering
in the exploding shells.

Peter

Helmed on deck, surveyor of the waves,
his shrewd gaze measured distances,
sized fishing grounds, judged
the balance of haul and catch,
knew what the hold could take,
the sea could lose.
Out on the current's drift he read
the tides, the language of the clouds,
sounded the deeps, brought his vessel
 safely home.

He lost a son to water. Desolate,
he grieved, but knew its ways,
its power to surprise and claim,
channelled pain in energy of faith
planted and tended in a sheltered space.

Now beached in a single room,
he floats in a different light,
his ship a bed adjusted to his needs,
raised or lowered as required,
pillows to support his head.
Blue gaze is clouded
but still holds the sea's iris,
speaks what he cannot say.

He takes his own soundings,
rocks quietly at anchor,
as quietly, in time, cuts loose,
drifts off, returns
while we smile, wave
from the shore.

Waiting
(for my mother)

You had always known
this day would come,
had swept the room ready
and planned what you must do,
but now the door flies open
to an empty room
and you are chilled
by its sudden draught,
the starkness
of the undivided light.

You pin the corners
of your smile, your dress,
your life,
with precise hands
try to maintain its poise,
to steady the mind's wandering,
choosing neat clothes
for the sheen and colour
grief has dulled.

At mealtime gatherings
you sit there at the table end
in the same place,
try to follow with your eyes
the to and fro of talk
across the room,
but their light is clouded
laughter echoes distantly,
the ends of talk
fly off:
you let them drift.

You must visit with him privately,
within the spaces of your mind,
lie beside the place he warmed
for over fifty years,
feel the weight of his tenderness,
the movement of his heart.

And in the slow hours
and the long light
of the winter afternoon,
dozing on the couch,
you will sense him
as you did the other day
open the door softly,
walk carefully so not
to wake you
to the fireside chair
and sit there
as your breathing slows
and pain subsides.

He will wait while you
recover strength and life
and though you later wake
to find an empty place,
you know that he was there
and will not let you grieve
for more than you can bear,
but leaves the lasting imprint
of his care, returned to you
in trust for your security.

Sotiris and Elene

Visitors have ushered in another age
of holiday prosperity
and some has filtered through to them
in new alliances,
some business opportunities,
a stretching of boundaries
that widened the old street
removed the trees with whitewashed trunks
that had flanked lives and meeting space
and stippled with their glancing green
long afternoons.

Old buildings block progress:
out comes the olive press,
old houses with their balconies,
up go new apartment blocks
and souvenir dispensaries,
bars with cheap beer
and Western menu choice.

The dark-clothed elderly,
sitting on door-steps after toil,
shading with still, shrunken shapes
the harsh light of the street,
linger at the edge of sight,
slowly fade to sepia, then disappear
before we realise they have gone.

Not quite; they wait on the sill
of his unconsciousness;
their dulled, unseeing, all-seeing eyes
leading him home to the farmed plot,
the bending backs, gnarled hands,
the midday clearing in the beating sun
filtered through olive leaves
as shadows stretch

I remember how they used to sing out in the fields
as they worked, brought in the crops.
I remember the singing.
That's gone.

Yes, and I remember the hunger,
the aches of grinding days, no medicine,
the dangers – don't forget the war,
the occupation years –
That was no holiday.

That's true too

And yet…

Now she is gone, sunk
in distraction, displaced,
back in mind to when she was
koritsi dressing for the *passeggiata,*
meeting of voices, eyes
in the fiesta square.

He is still here, for now,
gazing on a world that he
no longer knows and
carries on, indifferent.
He has less to say these days,
less to share, waits simply
for the easing of joints and mind
in opened glades,
ancient olives shading rest,
throats loosening in a forgotten song.

Their Presences

Strange how, even now, bunched shadow, half-
glimpsed on a stair, a cushion's dent,
deceives the eye, restores the cat, the dog
which died just weeks apart last spring,
tripped us hourly, padded in our space,
claimed care's daily portion, followed
with their reading eyes each move's significance.
Still-breathing shapes of memory shade dusty
silences, drape angles of the regulated day,
fold their soft weight in dark corners of the mind
to stumble our step with their abrupt reality.

Distance comforts with its long perspective,
small irritations fade in nostalgia's haze
which mutes the demanding voice, hoarse edge of bark,
that wet day, meal-time petulance, soothes
the restless energy, smoothes evidence
of scuffed floors, stained walls, clawed furniture.
And yet I miss their silent sharing of our space,
the active and the passive moods
of each day's partnership, miss
our need to balance movement to accommodate
their differences, their presences, to stretch
provision, make room, take account.

Becoming animal

Taking the lane that night
a little fast,
I turn, catch eye-shine
from a startled hind
that loose-limbed
bounds across the verge,
melts into mist and dark -
vanishes.
A held breath. Hush.
Pulse quickening.
We brush; here, now
our pace collides,
eyes briefly meet,
exchange alarm:
we do not know
each others' names.

I'll shed my coat,
my prison of brick, of metal
and of glass,
melt through the boundaries
of bone and skin
to find myself again
in your sleek hide,
your swift pace
and your startled gaze.

Can I enter the sharp currents
of your energy,
the stillness of your grazing pools,
enter your secret fellowship?
I am outside the forest,
on the wrong side of the riverbank,
and it is buttressed with fear.

Ted Hughes' Memorial

He is sleeping there
humped on a swell of moor
against the slow
passage of the cloud:
a granite metamorphosis.
Through the days' swing
his body feels
the stippling of rain,
the lichen's pigmenting,
feels the coarse grass
grazing his thighs,
a passing bird
perched on his brow
seeping its thin song.
His pulse sounds
in the throat
of buried streams,
muffles in earth
as letter gravings
weather, fade to air

The Sea's Burden

The sea has spread
and swallowed land through time,
Now it sways between continents,
keeps them strange.
From far shores it gathers histories,
consumes their slow accretions,
bears our wealth, our waste,
does not discriminate.
Its flux and flow answers
the patient cycle of the moon.

Sometimes it groans and sighs
with the secret weight it bears,
the stories drowned and folded in its deep.
Sometimes it heaves its burden
unexpectedly, stumbles the step
of a woman walking a Greek shore
with a child bleached to coral's bone
and rolled in brine.

What we cast out, the sea brings back.
Too young to walk or swim
the child was lifted, rocked
over distances, emptied finally
to pity or indifference.
She cradled, buried it as hers
while her lament
'Dead, dead, dead!'
fed the receding grind
of wave on stone.

The Carpenter of Lampedusa

Over years he read the grain in wood,
traced stories carved in rings,
tested its weight, its edge,
honed and planed and crafted it
to mould our comforts
and necessities.

Scouring the shore one day
eyes grazed wood splinters
flung by the tide's reach,
chipped paint, a vessel's
broken name.
Mind pieced the skeleton
of a journey ending here
in fractured hope,
spilt lives.
This wood was graved
with suffering; he saw it
labour on the waves,
heard its sinews crack.

He took some rough spars,
stroked them, hammered them
into a cross, an upturned hand,
left a protruding nail
in cross's arm, hand's palm,
to speak of sacrifice.
No comfort or necessity, now
a symbol cased in a museum cabinet
to frame a narrative
of exodus, of struggle,
and of loss.

The Sewing-circle

Printed with butterflies and flowers
in bedroom pastels
fleeces pile on floors
comfortable and carpeted
in suburban living-rooms:
a busyness of needlework
and women's neat dexterity,
bent head, quick eyes and fingers
cutting, measuring, securing,
fashioning to snuggle-bags
warm as our skin.

What can we do? the pictures
wring our minds; those
tiny bodies and bewildered eyes;
we can send them to the
cold shores where lives
spill with waves relentlessly,
where they can embrace
the smallest lives
like arms for a while.
It's something, not enough;
an offering.

Chemin

We pluck each day like ripe fruit
from the wayside trees,
each different, but fresh and sweet:
greengage pale green-golden
like the morning's eye,
mist bloom on pruneaux
deepening to purple as you rub the skin,
new pink of early figs slow-
plumped by the sun, each
savoured for succulence
and sustenance in southern light.
Earth unfolds and moulds
our trudging feet
across the limestone causse,
the sandy sentier, receives
the prints of soles and staff,
graved signatures of resolutions,
histories erased, remade by wind,
combed and crisped by seasons,
lifted and renewed, renewed,
renewed.

Movements in history

Wessex

Eyes in the reeds
watching, trained
on the distances,
twitch, rustle in the sedge.
King on the run,
a hunted beast
holed up, taut muscles,
panting heart.

Once he would meditate
within these spaces,
transcribe wisdom to the page,
quill scratching on parchment
through hours measured
by the candles' rings.
Now his kingdom is an island mere
brushed with water's silences.
The embellished faith of manuscript
lines his thin coat, warms the embers
of a rough hearth.

He is adrift, marooned;
vessels with their beaked prows
darken the sea's mouth.
Down here stems mesh, roots writhe,
eyes bore the gaps,
rustle, scrape of hidden voices,
splashes of long legs stalking shallows
haunt his sleep.

Where is hope? Will it return
on a merlin's wing?
His court has shrunk
to a sick child, a fretful wife
(and a daughter who may change things:
that's to come) – some loyal staff.
He will need to borrow
a beast's cunning and ruthlessness,
a leader's strategy.

He will depend on this,
this subtle shifting script
of water, reeds and sky.
It is his fortress, shield and page;
he is rooted in its knowing
and its patient time.
His palisade of leaves
will bend and close to conceal,
his moat mire the enemy,
part to his escape,
release.

He can read, translate Latin texts
into the people's tongue,
translate this too, knows that
with steadiness of mind, of arm,
this land will serve him
when the time is right,
will serve him well,
after darkness, anger
and the savage chase
will raise and cast him
shining on the flood.

A Knight and his Lady

This husband, wife, were floated
from another age upon a solemn bed,
angels kneeling at their heads,
softening stone pillows.
They lie recumbent, side by side
suspended in the vault of time
in attitudes of chivalry, obedience.
Exposed to view below the chapel's fretted sky,
ringed with the rustle of prayers,
they keep their privacy; they are covered
by the patient vigilance of saints.

The light of autumn afternoons
uncurls the stiffened lineaments
of honour, duty, stirs the marble
of the pleated robe,
lapped scales of mail.
There they remain as shadows
of each hour, day, year
revolve on their sleep.
They are stranded but not alone;
they have moulded a companionship,
one hand on a sword hilt,
one on folds of skirt.
He holds out a hand,
she places hers in his;
looped in a pledge of tenderness
together they outface the spaces,
the dark that settles
when the feet have left.

Brother Sun

Finally he sloughed the skin
of sickness,
woke on fine linen
to the grace of light
to be received by living day.
He had shed something else:
a former life, another memory
and now dwelt in an envelope of sun
that burnt his soul.

Through a casement
open on the ancient roofs
his new gaze focused
on a pecking bird
in humble brown.
From his convalescent bed
he reached a hand, saw
its bright black eye,
felt in his mind the brush
of feather, scale of leg,
moved in its tiny pulse.

Space
winged apart, contracted
to a wing or beak tip,
flower sepal, vein of leaf
and entered questing lives
beyond the walls of privilege.
Slowly silks slipped
to the floor, he folded
in a coarser cloak,
gilt browned to the rust
of tiles and trudging road,
leather shrunk to stone and skin.

Hands and feet carved
with new purpose,
he bore the ruby marks
of pain. The *celeste*
of rich brocades, of aristocracy
were now the palace walls
of sky, egg-shell delicate,
the promise of another
incarnation, other destiny:

Anima di Christo, santificami.
Corpo di Christo, salvami.
Sangue di Christo, inebriami
Acqua del costato di Christo, confortami.

Last of the Plantagenets

He was sculpted by history; its narrative
raised castles, crowns above his head,
scooped dungeons, flickering with treachery,
beneath his feet.
He was sealed in a dark place
ringed with speculation, whispering.
He was warped by poets' pens,
made to glower and limp on stage,
praised, reviled, for favour, fear,
mounted to heroic heights by loyalists.
The truth, as always very deep,
lies somewhere in between.

It was sleeping far below our passing feet,
the weight of vehicles, bruised
by the shifting plates of time.
Truth lay in the emptying of life
into a shrunken frame of bones
curled in a rough bed, the misshapen back,
the dented skull and other segments
pieced together then.

In his final progress through Leicester streets
bowed to his shadow, he borrowed grace
from his high-stepping horse,
wore the pride of lineage,
crested with valour, anticipated victory.

Years telescope, curl back to origins.
Now unfleshed, unseated,
he returns, the city's chastened son.
Shrunken to a box of bones
he is recognised, received,
lifted from ignominy
to new reverence, applause.

Shakespeare's Garden

Suddenly tired, answering the quieter
voice of age, time's chill messenger,
he steps back from applause, withdraws
from the hot light of stage publicity,
the sweeping arm, the shouting heart,
the medley massed ranks mouthing
their approval or dissent.

Suddenly tired, he withdraws, gratefully, at last,
into the wings of action and the streaming day
to curtain speech in a closed soliloquy.
Settling final dues, collecting his effects,
he takes his leave and rattles the rough road back
to Midlands' sedge and meadows' damp,
stands of old oaks, the plotted holdings
of the county wealth honouring the yeoman
and the merchant's dignity.

Tired, gladly he returns to ordinary solidity,
respectability, the honest pride of neighbours,
provincial accolades. Returns to root wealth
in the pride of New Place, planting the security
of old age in the turned, re-turned and tended ground.
And from its soil he cultivates the vine
which crops its fruit for all invited to participate
in summer's wealth of wine.

Grafting stem slips to the old stock
with a craftsman's patience the gardener of Stratford
listens for sap's rustle in the hidden veins
as life works its secret alchemy,
drives its energy to feed the final flowering,
startle with the clamour of its tongues of flame.
Thought flowing in the rhythm of the working hands,
he coaxes movement from sleep's lethargy,

trains and calms the sprawl of new growth
to fulfilled maturity.

Strength seeping weight in gradual
acceptance of the body's pain, he
settles to day's pendulum which swings
its slow light in the mind's room,
trusts the sweet, shed blood of the fruiting mulberry tree
will deepen the colour of his wine eventually.

On London's bustling, distant stage
Heminge and Condell of The King's Men
rifle through the guarded chest of theatre property,
struggle to sort and grade the fair and foul leaves
of imagination's flowering, sweep dispersed seeds
from crevices, empty the stuffed vessels of memory
to rescue a neglected treasury,
clutch them in a harvest gathering for us,
invite time's children to the celebration feast.

With neighbourly and modest courtesy
the gardener of New Place responded
to requests for cuttings, gardening advice,
never once imagining the fame
of Mr. Shakespeare's vines would spread
for twenty years or so beyond his death.

Moves in the Tudor Court

I. Henry Rex

Broad-shouldered, vigorous
he straddled the stage,
strode his manhood
for posterity.
Flushed with triumph,
he was Renaissance prince,
golden-haired
and radiant,
wore chivalry with elegance
and military nerve.
He mounted steeds
and charged into the lists,
with courtly assault
won ladies' favours
royally.

The blow, when it came,
was sudden, unforeseen;
from jousting champion
unseated, floored
and left for dead
beneath the horses' prance.
Fear whispers
swarmed around
the body on the ground
and sunk a darkness
in its heart.

When pumped to life
it mended unsteadily,
drove uneven rhythms
in the old securities,
lurched from calm

to anger, spite,
to flash of vengeance
punishing the confident,
smothering the dry cry
of his impotence
in empty nights.

II. Master Cromwell

Within the screened space
of the mind,
thought spider-fingering
a secret script
stretches its web
page over page,
closes with the faintest smile,
secures.

Shadows whisper,
stifle light,
laughter flutters,
falters,
trails to hush.

Courtiers trim sleeves
to fold and carry messages.
Strategy ticks
in panelled rooms,
suspicion, soft-soled,
stalks the passages.

He, Cromwell, in his study,
Holbein-robed,
holds in suspense
hope, fear,
shifts papers,
steadies hands,

turns his blue ring
from the cardinal,
warms visions on the flame
of memory.

A figure enters, shy
rustle of quills and fronds,
quiet as grace
moves through the ordered space.

One by one the trembling lights
are quenched by a still hand,
one after one,
noiseless as breath,
until the last, stark
handplay of firelight
on his watching face.

III. The Lady Anne

She fanned her cards
and played them, without looking,
dangerously,
distributed the ranks
to those who waited
on her favour,
thought she held
the power suits.

She wore her own fashion,
clasped her neck with velvet
and a drop pearl on fair skin,
chose new colours,
dared propriety.
She was slim as a peeled wand,
as a whip.

She studied a jewelled bible
in gloved hands,
traced its pieties,
studied how to serve
and rule.
Her features played
her subtleties;
she was mistress
and master,
bestowed smiles
sparingly.

Tied to her girdle
was the King, taut with desire,
floating letters on its flood,
turning songs for her delight:
The Lady Anne.
The Queen.

She cut the pack,
distributed her cards
And lost,
left with a barren hand
the promised gift
swaddled in blood,
blindfolded
and rolled in ash.

Eyes sharpened knives;
heads bent, waiting-ladies listened
as they plied their needlework.
Shadows swam from corners
to swamp her brief sun,
shiver the breath,
hang on her skirts
as she climbed steps

to the scaffold stage
of final theatre,
the sentence kiss of stone
and steel.

Lady Richmond's Ball, 15th June 1815

Candle gleam on Brussels lace and muslin
in the polished space,
crystal shimmer of the chandeliers,
glint of necklaces and keepsakes
on young skin,
prance and measure of dance steps
framed in elegance, precision
politesse.

Conversation tuned and turned with care
to compliments that heighten flush
in cheek and eye,
gloved hands steering others
to the nimble printing
of cotillion, quadrille.

Musicians carve their tunes,
quicken, waver, sink
to the tightened pathos
of the violin.
Outside the draped room,
light of lamps
is smudged
by rain's artillery
sharp on the panes.

An opened door.
Noise from the street:
a messenger.
In the pastel swirl
a figure tall and aquiline
in red and black
stoops to listen, quietly
unfolds the missive handed him.
Pause
chimed by the mantle clock.

Patterns dissolve,
doors swing apart.
The night pours in
and red sweeps out;
in file, dancers dreamwalk
through the raw hours
to the summoned lines
drenched and sleepless
in the pelting dark
of Waterloo.

Through the rising roar,
the smoking guns,
all meet unknown faces
drawn and stunned
in the half light,
grapple with steel and flesh
in mud,
struggle to a day that rises
on a trampled stage
of shredded colours, lives
ghosted to a wilderness
of dying cries.

Mary Shelley's Gift

Perfect, through stained with the struggle,
it lay beside her,
pride and prize of labour,
her first born.
She turned, murmured a name –
no answering cry, reached out –
limbs cold as pearl to her touch.
But in her dream she took it to the hearth
and rubbed skin with the fire's warmth
until the rose of life returned,
breath stirred.

She woke to morning and the memory of loss,
the ache and whiteness
of an empty crib,
no voice responding to a mother's
tenderness.

She had another dream:
a low, long room, dim light,
a table set with instruments
around a creature stretched there
born of stealth and sacrilege,
dismembered parts exhumed
at night and stitched
in secrecy.

Fired by ambition's energy,
convulsed by electricity, it
jerked to life upon an empty stage,
no ear to catch its first appeal,
no hand to lift or stroke shocked limbs
and scoop a refuge for the heart.

But this one had the strength
to take revenge.
Unravelling her birth tale
from the throes of nightmare,
she offered it to all creation's longing
as a bitter gift
and punishment.

Achterhuis

Skulk
like a mouse in the wainscot,
heart thudding
in the darkened corners of the room
at breath of danger,
step of predator.
Pause
with lifted foot
above the creaking stair:
there, take care,
don't move too soon.
Stifle laughter,
smother tears,
don't cough, don't sneeze,
don't breathe;
pricked ears
will pick you out,
the cat will pounce.

The days tick by.
The bells of Westerkerk next door
sound hours slowly,
measure the heart's heaviness,
their voices old and sonorous
but regular, reliable, till silenced
when their metal throats
are melted into cash for war.

Anger and desire contract
to an intensity
which carves its cursive narrative
on pages' aching space,
burns fire into the white,
whittles energy to hope
and vision's concentrated light.

The days revolve,
hand turns
on the turning page
as thought and character
unfold and find their space,
achieve a kind of grace
through pain.

Still the attic skylight
frames the stars,
the blue of spring and summer skies
beyond their touch or smell.
Dew shines and shivers
on the branches of the trees.
This can be seen sometimes;
two pairs of eyes can take it in:
life can be cradled in the hand
and wondered at.

Time grinds around
until the morning of discovery
that greets blank faces
paper white
and bodies starved of light.

The hand that ghosts
unrounded dreams
remains on blown
and scattered sheets
in the deserted cell,
moves through the years
and minds and consciences
of all those following.

Shostakovich

His mind was nerved to sound,
body strung to anxiety,
the jerky rhythms of unease.
Mistrusting mellow harmonies,
he tuned to discordances,
saw how the grind of locks, the
slam of steel, the blare
of sirens
was the music of the times.
But there was beauty
in dissonance,
the truth of the heart
that speech could not frame
and slid from the mouth,
emotion's lurch
that stopped the tongue.

His neck pricked with spies
that bored his art,
looked for disloyalties.
How could he plough a symphony
through fear? It smothered
spirit's pulse and lift.
Could he smuggle
through what he had seen
and knew,
could they translate his ironies?
Can irony of notes in any case
redeem the failure of the tongue?

He used to await
the summons for dissent,
alert all night with suitcase packed.
It never came.
But they controlled him nonetheless.

It might have been more simple
to die young with integrity intact
instead of through a life
secured in half-
truths, compromise.
Could music save his soul?
He wanted to articulate
and not disguise the pain;
could hope the stifled wail
might break out,
the muffled ticking of a Trio base
disrupt complacencies
and cheerful climaxes
in patient time.

His mind burned, fingers itched
to find the key to sound
the perfect triad chime
of conscience, life and craft.

Indigo Dreams Publishing Ltd
24, Forest Houses
Cookworthy Moor
Halwill
Beaworthy
Devon
EX21 5UU
www.indigodreams.co.uk